I'm a Christian— now what?

Written by
Andrea Brock Denton

100 Devotions for Girls

978-1-4336-8567-5

Published by B&H Publishing Group
Nashville, Tennessee

Dewey Decimal Classification: 242.62
Subject Heading: GIRLS \ CHRISTIAN LIFE \ DEVOTIONAL
LITERATURE

1 2 3 4 5 6 · 18 17 16 15

Contents

Introduction 1

1. Expect Nothing in Return. 2

2. Insults 4

3. Love Your Enemies. 6

4. Genuine Love 8

5. Honor One Another 10

6. Be Diligent 12

7. Keep On. 14

8. Talk to God 16

9. You Are Not Your Own 18

10. Go to Church. 20

11. A Strong Student Ministry 22

12. The Company You Keep 24

13. The Aroma of Christ 26

14. Transformed 28

15. Be Careful with Your Heart. 30

16. Set Apart 32

17. Life from the Word 34

18. Follow the Holy Spirit. 36

19. Be Responsible 38

20. Carry One Another 40

21. Be Helpful. 42

22. Decisions 44

23. Big Picture 46

24. Walk 48

25. Grace Others with Your Words..................... 50

26. Forgive 52

27. Live as a Child of Light.......................... 54

28. Expose Darkness 56

29. Your Future Husband 58

30. Live Worthy of the Gospel........................ 60

31. Put Others First 62

32. Shine 64

33. Become Wise 66

34. Walk in Him 68

35. Sound Theology 70

36. Think on Things Above 72

37. Hand Over Your Anger 74

38. Do Not Lie....................................... 76

39. Be Kind 78

40. Accept and Forgive 80

41. Peace... 82

42. Prayer.. 84

43. Love Everyone................................... 86

44. Rejection 88

45. Suit Up 90

46. Remember and Practice 92

47. Get Busy with Your Own Life 94

48. Who Are You Responsible For?................... 96

49. Tell the Future Generations 98

50. There Are Two Paths............................. 100

51. Embrace Discipline 102

52. Guard Your Heart 104

53. Train 106

54. Content 108

55. Content with Less 110

56. Pursue the Godly 112

57. Hope in God 114

58. Be Generous 116

59. Fearless 118

60. Pursue Righteousness 120

61. Keeping the End in Sight 122

62. Reserve Your Water 124

63. A Girl of Few Words 126

64. Slow to Anger 128

65. Apply What You Hear 130

66. Anti-Pollution 132

67. Merciful 134

68. Faith with Works 136

69. The Tongue 138

70. From Bitter to Sweet 140

71. Made in God's Likeness 142

72. Order 144

73. You Are Not of the World 146

74. The Spirit Speaks 148

75. Never Return to Your Old Ways 150

76. Treated with Honor 152

77. Give a Blessing 154

78. Be Ready 156

79. Be Perfect 158

80. Love One Another 160

81. Produce Fruit 162

82. Truth 164

83. In the Safari 166

84. Walk Like Christ 168

85. Walk in the Light 170

86. Love with Action 172

87. Keep God's Commands 174

88. Listen to the Lord 176

89. True Happiness 178

90. Study 180

91. How to Have a Full Life 182

92. You Are Remarkable 184

93. Silence 186

94. Don't Look Like a Pig 188

95. Build Your Reputation 190

96. Your Steps 192

97. Your Motives 194

98. My Daily Bread 196

99. Your Heart 198

100. Benediction 200

Introduction

Congratulations on making the biggest and best decision of your life! You have chosen to follow Jesus Christ, and you have a lot to look forward to, so much to learn, and so many blessings. He has big plans for you, and I hope these 100 Scriptures and devos will help guide you as you choose to give each new day to Him. Arm yourself with the Bible, pray through every challenge, and watch yourself grow closer to God each day.

You've done it. You're a Christian. Great! Now what? Now this . . .

Expect Nothing in Return

But love your enemies, do what is good, and lend, expecting nothing in return. Then your reward will be great, and you will be sons of the Most High. For He is gracious to the ungrateful and evil. Be merciful, just as your Father also is merciful.

—LUKE 6:35–36

Before these two verses, Luke mentions how it is easy to love those who love us in return, to be good to those who are good to us in return, and to loan to those who we know will repay us. But, the Gospel calls us to love, do good, and provide for others even if they do not love us, treat us well, or provide for us in return. The reason we are called to live this way is because Christ loves us even when we are unloving, He is good to us even when we are ungrateful, and He provides for us although we have nothing to offer Him. Christ loves expecting nothing in return; therefore, we are to love others with such mercy.

Who in your life loves you even when you're hard to love?

_____

_____

_____

_____

_____

_____

_____

_____

_____

_____

_____

_____

_____

_____

Insults

"You are blessed when they insult and persecute you and falsely say every kind of evil against you because of Me."

—MATTHEW 5:11

There will be times when people are unkind to you because you are a Christian. Christ tells us to consider ourselves blessed when this happens. Most of the time, we want to feel sorry for ourselves when people say mean things about us; but Christ shows us that when those comments are made because of what we believe, then we should consider ourselves blessed. The greater blessing is being in a relationship with the Lord, not receiving someone else's approval for what we believe.

Has anyone been unkind to you because you're a Christian?

_____

_____

_____

_____

_____

_____

_____

_____

_____

_____

_____

_____

_____

_____

Love Your Enemies

"You have heard that it was said, Love your neighbor and hate your enemy. But I tell you, love your enemies and pray for those who persecute you, so that you may be sons of your Father in heaven."

—MATTHEW 5:43–45

One of the hardest things to do is be nice to someone who is cruel to us. Yet, this is what God calls us to do. Christ says to love our enemies, but what does that look like? The command to love our enemies does not mean becoming BFFs with them. If someone (usually at your age it is a girl) has really hurt us, we should check our heart and make sure we are not harboring bad thoughts or feelings toward her, but we do not have to invite her to a sleepover. We can love her from a distance. For example, we can pray for her when God brings her to mind.

It seems impossible to love people who are mean to us, but when we stop and look at what Christ did for us, when we were His enemies, we realize that not only is it possible to love mean people, it is really the least we can do because of what has been done for us.

What are some ways you can show love to
people you might think of as "enemies"?

_____

_____

_____

_____

_____

_____

_____

_____

_____

_____

_____

_____

Genuine Love

Love must be without hypocrisy.
Detest evil; cling to what is good.

—ROMANS 12:9

It is hypocritical if we say we love our mom then talk poorly about her to our friends. It is hypocritical if we say we love our siblings but do not have their backs at school when someone picks on them. Genuine love is holding our tongue when we want to say something negative about someone we love, and it is standing up for those we love. If we say we love someone, we need to genuinely love that person by having our actions back up the love we profess for him or her.

What's your definition of *love*?

_____

_____

_____

_____

_____

_____

_____

_____

_____

_____

_____

_____

_____

Honor One Another

**Show family affection to one another with brotherly love.
Outdo one another in showing honor.**

—ROMANS 12:10

If you have a loving family, then you know what it is to give and receive "family affection." A smile crosses your face when you remember your family vacations, holiday traditions, and weekly family routines from meals at the dinner table to movie nights. The common thread to those memories is love. God tells us to love other people with the same love we experience in our families.

No family is perfect, but loving families go behind themselves and clean up any relational mess that is made. Correcting the mess you make within your family is just one way of honoring your family members. God calls His children to show this type of affection and honor outside, as well as inside, of their homes.

Do you need to clean up any relational mess
with a friend or family member?

Be Diligent

Do not lack diligence; be fervent in spirit; serve the Lord.

—ROMANS 12:11

Not only are we to love our families and others with family affection, we are to love the Lord in the same way. Christians love and honor the Lord by serving Him. At your age, you can serve God by honoring your parents, your other family members, your teachers, and your coaches. Some practical ways you can serve God are helping around your house (for no allowance!), going on mission trips with your youth group, not gossiping, and being grateful. Remember you do these things not to *be* loved by God but because you *are* loved by God.

Write a list of practical ways you can show your love for your family and for God.

_____

_____

_____

_____

_____

_____

_____

_____

_____

_____

_____

_____

Keep On

**Rejoice in hope; be patient in affliction;
be persistent in prayer. Share with the saints
in their needs; pursue hospitality.**

—ROMANS 12:12–13

In my work with preteen girls, I have discovered that relationships, usually with other girls, cause them the most difficulty in life. You know the drill—someone you thought was a friend turns out not to be, someone posts something personal about you, someone starts a rumor about you, you do not get invited to the slumber party, the friend you had at the beginning of seventh grade is not the same person in eight grade. Scripture encourages us in these times to be patient. Be patient as you wait on others around you to mature, rejoice in the hope that they will mature, and be persistent in prayer as you mature and maneuver through these years.

Do you have a friendship that you need to pray about?

_____

_____

_____

_____

_____

_____

_____

_____

_____

_____

_____

_____

_____

_____

_____

_____

Talk to God

I cry aloud to the LORD, and He answers me from His holy mountain.

—PSALM 3:4

Think about your closest friend. How often do you talk with her? Probably not a lot of time exists between your conversations. Good friends like to hear about each other's adventures, struggles, hopes, and dreams. In the same way, God wants to hear about our hopes, fears, dreams, and struggles. When we talk to God, He listens and answers. Sometimes the answers are immediate. Other times they are not. Sometimes God answers with a "yes," and other times He answers with a "no." His answers always have our best interest in mind, but to hear Him, we have to learn to listen for His voice. God speaks to us from Genesis to Revelation, and just like we know the voice of a good friend because of time spent with her, we must spend time reading God's Word in order to hear His voice.

Describe a time when God answered your prayers.

_____

_____

_____

_____

_____

_____

_____

_____

_____

_____

_____

_____

_____

_____

You Are Not Your Own

**Don't you know that your body is a sanctuary
of the Holy Spirit who is in you, whom you have from God?
You are not your own, for you were bought at a price.
Therefore glorify God in your body.**

—1 CORINTHIANS 6:19–20

In Old Testament times, God dwelled with His people in the tabernacle. The tabernacle was a place of worship for the Israelites. They would set up the tabernacle wherever they camped because it was their sanctuary. It was how God met with them. Presently, God meets with His people through Jesus. The tabernacle no longer exists because Christ's death and resurrection allows God to dwell with His people. The Holy Spirit dwells in those who have accepted Christ as their Lord and Savior, and their bodies are God's sanctuary.

God lives in you since you are a Christian! Since the almighty, holy, and perfect God tabernacles in you, you should keep His sanctuary—your body—pure, holy, and blameless.

Since your body is God's sanctuary, how should you treat it?

_____
_____
_____
_____
_____
_____
_____
_____
_____
_____
_____
_____
_____
_____

Go to Church

And they devoted themselves to the apostles' teaching, to the fellowship, to the breaking of bread, and to the prayers.

—ACTS 2:42

A Christian needs to be part of a Bible believing, Christ-centered church. If you are not already in a church community, do some research and visit some churches. If your parents cannot take you to church, then ask some of your other friends who are Christians if you can visit their churches. A church is where you will be taught God's Word, have fellowship with other Christians, remember Christ's death and resurrection, look forward to Christ's return, and be prayed for by other believers. Whether you are visiting a church or already actively involved in a church, check out the student ministry of the church so you can also plug in to the church with students your own age.

What do you like about your church or the
church you are visiting?

_____

_____

_____

_____

_____

_____

_____

_____

_____

_____

_____

_____

_____

11

A Strong Student Ministry

So the body is not one part but many. . . . But now God has placed each one of the parts in one body just as He wanted. And if they were all the same part, where would the body be?

—1 CORINTHIANS 12:14, 18–19

This passage is talking about the church. A youth group cannot and should not replace the church, but think about your youth group right now. If members spent their time wishing they were someone other than who God designed them to be, then the youth group would not properly reflect God. If your foot decided to stop being a foot because it wished it were a hand instead, how would you walk?

When students are growing in their own walk with the Lord rather than focusing on what other students in the ministry are doing, then they reflect God to their community.

Do not waste your time wishing you were a hand if you are a foot. Instead spend time developing your talents so God can be reflected through your life.

What are your gifts? How can you use them?

The Company You Keep

Do not be deceived: "Bad company corrupts good morals."

—1 CORINTHIANS 15:33

I have worked with middle and high school students for my entire adult life. When I see students making bad choices, it is without fail the result of them hanging around friends who are a bad influence on them. We like to think that we are mentally, emotionally, and socially strong to be friends with whoever we want, but the truth is we all succumb to temptation when we are keeping friends in our inner circle who sway us into walking down the wrong path.

Think about your closest friends. What good
ways do they influence you?

The Aroma of Christ

But thanks be to God, who always puts us on display in Christ and through us spreads the aroma of the knowledge of Him in every place. For to God we are the fragrance of Christ among those who are being saved and among those who are perishing.

—2 CORINTHIANS 2:14–15

I remember being a little girl and loving the smell of my mom's perfume. It was a subtle, distinct, sweet scent. If she would hug me bye while wearing her perfume, I would catch whiffs of her aroma on me while we were apart. Even now as a grown woman, I still know my mom's scent. When she leaves my home after a visit, even my children will walk into the room where she stayed and say, "I smell Pebby" (their name for their grandmother). This is exactly what Christ wants of us. He wants to be so close to us in friendship that we begin to smell like Him. He wants others to get a whiff of Him from their interactions with us, and when we part ways with others, He wants us to leave a pleasant aroma of what it is to walk with God.

When you spend time with others, do you remind them of Christ?

_____

_____

_____

_____

_____

_____

_____

_____

_____

_____

_____

_____

_____

_____

Transformed

**We all, with unveiled faces, are looking as in a mirror
at the glory of the Lord and are being transformed
into the same image from glory to glory;
this is from the Lord who is the Spirit.**

—2 CORINTHIANS 3:18

A few verses before this verse, Paul, the author of 2 Corinthians, writes about Moses' veiled face. Moses would put a veil over his face after meeting with the Lord because his face would shine from having been in the presence of the Lord. He would hide his radiant face from the Israelites because they did not have sunglasses to put on to block the rays of light coming off of Moses. The veil would also keep the Israelites from seeing his radiance fade away.

God had a special relationship with Moses. He would speak to Moses and then have Moses communicate His words to the Israelites. Today, God meets with us just as He once met with Moses, but our meeting with God happens through the Holy Spirit. The Holy Spirit transforms us more and more into the image of Christ, and we are given a radiance that will never fade.

How can you shine His light in the world?

15

Be Careful with Your Heart

Do not be mismatched with unbelievers. For what partnership
is there between righteousness and lawlessness?
Or what fellowship does light have with darkness?

—2 CORINTHIANS 6:14

Think about the future family you want, the mom you want to be, and the kind of man you want to marry. Is arguing with your husband about you taking your children to church, and him not wanting you to, anywhere in that picture? Marriage is one of many ways we can partner ourselves with unbelievers. God gives us a warning in this passage about blending ourselves with others who do not believe in Him. He lets us know that it is like trying to mix oil and water. It is a mix of light and darkness that leaves the relationship lop-sided. A mismatched partnership would be like seesawing. When one person is up, the other would be down. There would never be a balance.

Aim to let the people who speak into your life and influence you be people who believe in the death and resurrection of Christ. You might have different tastes in music, different political views, and different opinions on an array of topics, but you will follow the same Lord.

Make a list of the characteristics that make a good husband or wife.

Set Apart

Therefore, dear friends, since we have such promises, let us cleanse ourselves from every impurity of the flesh and spirit, completing our sanctification in the fear of God.

—2 CORINTHIANS 7:1

The promises in 2 Corinthians 7:1 are the same promises God has spoken since the call of Abraham in Genesis 12. God promises to be God and Father to His people. He will take care of us, and we will be His sons and daughters. Paul says that since we have such a promise of being family with God, then we should clean up our act. The holiest of beings is our Father. If you have a healthy relationship with your dad, you most likely want to be on your best behavior around him out of respect for him. In the same manner, we should clean up our hearts and minds out of respect for our heavenly Father. Unlike our earthly dads, God is always with us, which means we should always want to act our best, and God is perfect, which means we are called to more than just being nice. God calls us to be set apart. There should be a distinct difference between us and the world because we serve a holy God.

What makes it hard to look different from the world?

_____

_____

_____

_____

_____

_____

_____

_____

_____

_____

_____

_____

_____

Life from the Word

The instruction of the LORD is perfect, renewing one's life; the testimony of the LORD is trustworthy, making the inexperienced wise. The precepts of the LORD are right, making the heart glad; the command of the LORD is radiant, making the eyes light up.

—PSALM 19:7-8

The synonyms used for God's Word in these verses are instruction, testimony, precepts, and command of the Lord. The Bible instructs us how to live; it gives us eyewitness accounts of many of the events it describes; and it gives us understanding. The adjectives used to describe God's Word in these verses are perfect, trustworthy, right, and radiant. Psalm 19:7–8 also tells us what God's Word does for us. Scripture renews us, makes us wise, makes our hearts glad, and fills our eyes with light. Being in God's Word has an internal and external effect on us. We literally change from the inside out when we allow the Word of God to penetrate our hearts.

Choose a favorite verse, and write it below. Can you memorize it?

_____

_____

_____

_____

_____

_____

_____

_____

_____

_____

_____

_____

_____

_____

18

Follow the Holy Spirit

Now those who belong to Christ Jesus have crucified the flesh with its passions and desires. Since we live by the Spirit, we must also follow the Spirit.

—GALATIANS 5:24–25

Living by the Spirit means not satisfying the desires of our sinful nature. We are to run in the opposite direction when we have the desire to gossip, lie, steal, cheat, be mean, or think mean thoughts. Following the Spirit means putting as much distance between us and the things that tempt us. If we are tempted to be cruel on social media, then we should stop using it. If we are having mean thoughts or lying, then we might need to stop hanging around certain friends or watching shows that have a bad influence on us.

Take a look at your life. Where are you prone to temptation? Ask Christ to show you what it looks like to crucify those desires and then ask Him to help you rid yourself of those desires.

Which temptations are the hardest for you to fight?

Be Responsible

For each person will have to carry his own load.

—GALATIANS 6:5

I studied abroad when I was in college. In the pre-trip meetings, my professors stressed to the group to pack only what we could carry. Packing light for three months required some strategic planning. The idea of packing only what you can carry teaches responsibility. If a person cannot carry his or her own load, then it requires someone else to step in. When we are responsible for our own selves, it keeps others from having to be responsible for us. When each member of a family, each employee of a company, or each student in a class is responsible, then there is more time and energy to invest in important matters rather than picking up each other's slack.

What are some ways you could be more responsible?

_____

_____

_____

_____

_____

_____

_____

_____

_____

_____

_____

_____

_____

_____

Carry One Another

Carry one another's burdens; in this way you will fulfill the law of Christ.

—GALATIANS 6:2

Notice what this verse does not say. It does not say to sit back and allow someone else to carry your burdens. Do not live with the assumption that others will pick up your burdens, but do pick up theirs. Be responsible for yourself, and at the same time, help others. Carry your own load, and out of a concerned heart for others, carry their load. This can look like listening, sending a quick text of encouragement, actually writing and sending a note, praying, or lending a helping hand. When we look outside of our selves and our own circumstances, we become more Christlike.

Who do you know who eagerly helps others? Does that person remind you of Christ?

Be Helpful

Therefore, as we have opportunity, we must work for the good of all, especially for those who belong to the household of faith.

—GALATIANS 6:10

There are so many opportunities to serve in a church. As you get to know other families in your church, you will see those opportunities. Look at how God has gifted you, pray for how you might serve those in your church and community, and then watch. You might end up visiting an elderly couple once a week, helping a widow around her house or in her yard, baking treats for someone in the hospital, babysitting for a particular family in need of extra help, being a mentor to a younger girl, tutoring a younger student in your favorite subject, or teaching someone one of your skills. Watch and see how God will use you for the good of those in your church and community.

Make a list of ten ways you can serve God by serving others. Which one can you do this week?

_____

_____

_____

_____

_____

_____

_____

_____

_____

_____

_____

_____

_____

Decisions

**Who is the man who fears the LORD?
He will show him the way he should choose.**

—PSALM 25:12

Some choices are easier than others. In all of your choices, God is by your side. He will show you the right choice to make because you fear Him. To fear the Lord means you have a good relationship with Him. In your closest friendships, you know what the other person is thinking or feeling because you are in touch with that person. You talk and hang out frequently. You learn what that person likes and dislikes. In the same way, you will know what God desires when you are close to Him. He will teach you His ways and help you with the decisions you have to make.

Are you in the middle of having to make a hard decision or choice?

_____

_____

_____

_____

_____

_____

_____

_____

_____

_____

_____

_____

_____

23

Big Picture

**Do not be agitated by evildoers;
do not envy those who do wrong. For they wither
quickly like grass and wilt like tender green plants.**

—PSALM 37:1–2

It is easy to get caught up in what seems unfair. Your teacher might call you out for your behavior while another student who is acting worse gets away with his behavior because the teacher did not see him but did see you. Let's take the scenario a step further and say the student who did not get in trouble is a bully. Scripture says not to let the injustices you see bother you because the bully will wither away. It may not be this school year, but you will see the bully's power shrivel. Do not envy mean people who sometimes get away with mean things. Their meanness may not fade, but the imbalance of their power will diminish.

Have you ever known someone who was a bully but later changed?

_____

_____

_____

_____

_____

_____

_____

_____

_____

_____

_____

_____

_____

Walk

**And you were dead in your trespasses and sins
in which you previously walked according to the ways of this
world, according to the ruler who exercises authority over the
lower heavens, the spirit now working in the disobedient.**

—EPHESIANS 2:1–2

The world tells us to be selfish, to look out for ourselves, and to do what feels good. The world tells us, as females, to expose our femininity and leave nothing up to the masculine imagination.

The path of the world is the path you were on before Christ. As a Christian, you no longer follow that path. That path is in your past, and you now walk on the path of obedience to Christ because you have been given the gift of eternal life.

How has your acceptance of Christ changed
your path?

Grace Others with Your Words

**No foul language is to come from your mouth,
but only what is good for building up someone in need,
so that it gives grace to those who hear.**

—EPHESIANS 4:29

Foul language entails more than just cussing. It is anything that tears others down. That includes gossiping and put-downs. Think about your conversations. Would you have most of them in front of other people? If your answer to that question is "no," then you should probably stop those conversations before they happen. As a Christian, your words should bring beauty and ease to others, not hurt.

As a teacher, I find that the female students are tempted with foul language in the girls' bathroom, at lunch, and behind any screen associated with technology. Are your words in those places uplifting others or tearing them down?

Do you talk differently depending on whom you're around?

Forgive

And be kind and compassionate to one another, forgiving one another, just as God also forgave you in Christ.

—EPHESIANS 4:32

When others cause us pain, it is easy to dislike them or write them off, but it is hard to forgive them. It is hard to get over pain that someone else caused us, yet God calls us to do so. How can we just move on from the hurt and forget that it ever happened? This verse gives us the answer. Christ forgave us so we must forgive one another. Whatever someone does to cause us pain cannot compare to what we did to Christ. We put Christ on the cross. Our sin put Him there. Remembering how Christ forgave us of the greatest pain possible, our sin, helps us put forgiveness in perspective. We can forgive others of their wrongs because Christ has forgiven us of ours, and what we did to Christ far outweighs what anyone has done to us.

Why do you think forgiveness is sometimes so hard for us?

Live as a Child of Light

For you were once darkness, but now you are light in the Lord. Walk as children of light—for the fruit of the light results in all goodness, righteousness, and truth—discerning what is pleasing to the Lord.

—EPHESIANS 5:8–10

Light bulbs are not lit when we buy them. We have to take them home, screw them into a light socket, and then flip the switch that controls them in order for them to shine light. Before accepting Christ, you were like a light bulb on the shelf at the store. You were unlit, but because you accepted Christ, you now shine. The switch has been flipped. Justice, honesty, and truth should flow out of the light you shine. These things please the Lord, the source of your light.

How do you shine differently now than before you became a Christian?

Expose Darkness

Don't participate in the fruitless works of darkness, but instead expose them.

—EPHESIANS 5:11

Sometimes when you get caught up in trying to be someone you are not, you do not recognize that talking about others, snickering at others, and saving seats for some but not others is a waste of time and energy. These types of mean behavior are dark, futile, and pointless. They do no one good. As a Christian, you are told not to join in such pathetic behavior. In fact, you should expose such behavior. Now, revealing meanness may not win you any popularity votes, but you are called to behave based on how God views you, not on how others view you.

Have you witnessed mean behavior in the last few weeks? If so, what did you do?

_____

_____

_____

_____

_____

_____

_____

_____

_____

_____

_____

_____

_____

Your Future Husband

Husbands, love your wives, just as Christ loved the church and gave Himself for her.

—EPHESIANS 5:25

You are not too young to start praying for your future husband. When you pray for him, you want to pray that he will love you as Christ loved the church, giving His life for you as Christ gave His life for the church. Your role in your future marriage is to submit, or yield, to your husband. This will not be difficult to do when a man loves you as Christ loved the church. Wait on such a man! Pray for such a man!

What are the benefits of marrying a Christian?

Live Worthy of the Gospel

Just one thing: Live your life in a manner worthy of the gospel of Christ.

—PHILIPPIANS 1:27

If you play a sport, think of the pride you feel when you wear your jersey, especially if your team in on a winning streak. If you play for your school, think about how your coaches stress that you represent your school even when you are not wearing your jersey. Think about the academic and behavioral standards you have to meet in order to be on the team. As a Christian, you are on God's team. You play for and represent Him. As a player on His team, you are to live, speak, dress, and think in a way that honors Him.

In context, this verse is saying to live worthy of the gospel, not just individually, but as a group of believers who are united as one just like players on a court or field are instructed to play selflessly and as one team. Christians should together as one team live selflessly, honor the Lord, and wear their team jersey with pride.

If God's team had a motto, what would it be?

_____

_____

_____

_____

_____

_____

_____

_____

_____

_____

_____

_____

_____

_____

Put Others First

**Do nothing out of rivalry or conceit,
but in humility consider others as more important
than yourselves. Everyone should look out not only
for his own interests, but also for the interests of others.**

—PHILIPPIANS 2:3–4

Jesus left us with a beautiful picture of humility when He washed the disciples' feet. He knelt down and served them by cleaning the dirtiest part of their bodies, and after washing their feet, He told them to serve one another.

Jesus knows that serving one another makes strong relationships, homes, and communities. He desires that we serve those people He places right in front of us—our family and our friends. We are to view them as more important than ourselves. Rather than acting superior to our siblings, we should humbly place them above ourselves. Rather than competing out of jealousy, we should serve. Rather than snubbing someone out of pride, we should consider her better than ourselves.

When was the last time you served someone else? How did it make you feel?

_____

_____

_____

_____

_____

_____

_____

_____

_____

_____

_____

_____

_____

_____

Shine

**Do everything without grumbling and arguing,
so that you may be blameless and pure, children of God
who are faultless in a crooked and perverted generation,
among whom you shine like stars in the world.**

—PHILIPPIANS 2:14–15

I love how miniature clear lights light up a Christmas tree in a darkened room. I also love how bright stars ignite a black night sky. These are both great visuals to how a Christian should light the world around her. One way to shine the light of Christ is by not complaining or arguing. Think of how this would change our families alone. Can you imagine the change in our homes from no complaints to parents, no arguments with parents, and no arguments with our siblings?

What do you complain about?

_____

_____

_____

_____

_____

_____

_____

_____

_____

_____

_____

_____

_____

_____

Become Wise

**The fear of the LORD is the beginning of knowledge;
fools despise wisdom and discipline.**

—PROVERBS 1:7

One of the synonyms Psalm 19:9 uses for God's Word is the phrase "fear of the LORD." Here in Proverbs 1:7, we read that "fear of the LORD," or God's Word, is the beginning of knowledge. Reading the Bible is the beginning of knowledge, wisdom, and discipline. We can turn to schools and education for knowledge, but the only place to base and test that knowledge is the Bible. God's Word teaches, guides, and corrects us. In order to benefit from its instructions, we must read it.

Fill in the blank: "My Bible is _____." Why did you choose that answer?

_____

_____

_____

_____

_____

_____

_____

_____

_____

_____

_____

_____

_____

_____

Walk in Him

Therefore, as you have received Christ Jesus the Lord, walk in Him, rooted and built up in Him and established in the faith, just as you were taught, overflowing with gratitude.

—COLOSSIANS 2:6–7

I enjoy running and love participating in races. The point of a race is to stay on course and finish. It would be pointless to run a different path than the racecourse. You would miss the finish line.

Imagine Christ as the racecourse of life and living with Him in eternity as the finish line. You want to walk and run in Him, the path. Staying in Christ causes growth and gratitude, and being founded in Him gets you to the finish line. In this scenario, the finish line is just the beginning of life not the end.

What does it look like to walk in Christ?

Sound Theology

Be careful that no one takes you captive through philosophy and empty deceit based on human tradition, based on the elemental forces of the world, and not based on Christ.

—COLOSSIANS 2:8

It is important to join a church that teaches the Bible as the authoritative Word of God. A church, that believes God's Word is authoritative, is a church that teaches God's Word is over and above any other teaching. God's Word is trustworthy, and it influences how we view God, mankind, and the world. Make sure you are being taught this truth and not deceitful imitations.

How do you know if a church teaches the truth?

Think on Things Above

So if you have been raised with the Messiah, seek what is above, where the Messiah is, seated at the right hand of God. Set your minds on what is above, not on what is on the earth.

—COLOSSIANS 3:1–2

Accepting Christ means we believe in His death and resurrection. He died a death that we deserve, paying the penalty for sin. He also conquered death when He rose from the grave three days after dying. For us, Christ died to satisfy God's punishment for sin, and He gave us the promise of resurrection when He returns. We die to the ways of the world because we have the hope of being with Christ in heaven one day. It is out of that hope that we are to think about heavenly things and not get caught up in worldly things.

What makes you happier—thinking about heavenly things or worldly things?

_____

_____

_____

_____

_____

_____

_____

_____

_____

_____

_____

_____

_____

Hand Over Your Anger

But now you must also put away all the following: anger, wrath, malice, slander, and filthy language from your mouth.

—COLOSSIANS 3:8

Have you ever looked at the root cause of something mean you did? Looking at what causes you to act mean can help you place your meanness in the hands of Christ. Maybe you were nasty to someone because you did not feel heard, your feelings were hurt, or the person was just an easy target. When we keep hatred or irritation in our hearts, anger flows out of us, and it usually comes out through our words. Our tongues can insult, cuss, and cause pain. When we hand Christ our anger and irritabilities, He dissolves them all.

What are practical ways to hand over your anger to God?

Do Not Lie

Do not lie to one another, since you have put off the old self with its practices.

—COLOSSIANS 3:9

Cancer is a horrible disease that attacks the body. Cancer can impact an entire family and community, but the cancer itself only affects the cancer patient. As the disease grows in the patient's body, the patient is weakened from the sickness. One way to rid the body of the cancer is to undergo treatments that reach every place in the body where the cancer has spread. Think of lying like cancer. Your lies can impact those around you, but really they are only affecting you as they cause havoc inside of you. The only way to rid your life of lying is to undergo the treatment of truth. Speak the truth even when it means you may get in trouble. Being grounded to help you learn the importance of telling the truth far outweighs being eaten up inside with lies.

Is there anything that you need to be truthful about?

_____

_____

_____

_____

_____

_____

_____

_____

_____

_____

_____

_____

_____

Be Kind

Therefore, God's chosen ones, holy and loved, put on heartfelt compassion, kindness, humility, gentleness, and patience.

—COLOSSIANS 3:12

Being a Christian means you are to live a holy life. To be holy means to be "set apart." What better sets you apart from a world filled with hate than to love? You are called to be compassionate, kind, humble, gentle, and patient.

When you are riding in the car with a parent, do you see a lot of compassion, kindness, and patience from other drivers? Probably not. This world is filled with selfishness, harshness, and impatience. You can witness this just by driving around town or on the interstate. As a Christian, you are called to steer your life differently. Rather than cutting in front of people and racing to get ahead, set yourself apart by loving others well and treating them with kindness.

How often do you feel set apart from the world?

Accept and Forgive

Accepting one another and forgiving one another if anyone has a complaint against another. Just as the Lord has forgiven you, so you must also forgive.

—COLOSSIANS 3:13

This verse picks up midsentence from Colossians 3:12, which is about being kind. What helps us love and be kind is when we accept others for who they are and forgive them for how they can behave. When we get to know the story of someone's life, it helps us accept them just as they are and forgive them if need be. Remember our standard to accept and forgive others is God. God accepts us just as we are, and He forgives us of the greatest offense. Just as He has forgiven us, so we must also forgive.

Do you have any old grudges that need to be forgiven?

_____

_____

_____

_____

_____

_____

_____

_____

_____

_____

_____

_____

_____

Peace

**And let the peace of the Messiah, to which you were
also called in one body, control your hearts. Be thankful.**

—COLOSSIANS 3:15

A lot can control our hearts—a story that we read or
watch, an emotion, a crush, determination, jealousy,
the list goes on and on. God tells us in His Word to allow
His peace to control our hearts. Peace is genuine. We
cannot fake peace. We either have it or we do not. If
peace is in our hearts, it reigns over all of our thoughts
and feelings, and we are overcome with thanks. Pray for
the peace of Christ to rule your heart.

Describe a moment when you felt the most peaceful.

42

Prayer

Devote yourselves to prayer; stay alert in it with thanksgiving.

—COLOSSIANS 4:2

Where do you invest your time and energy? Are you devoted to excelling academically, in a certain sport, or in the fine arts? If you are, you know the time and practice that it requires of you. The same is true about prayer. Devoting yourself to prayer demands your time and your energy. It also requires dedicating yourself to the practice of prayer. As you pray, stay alert to what you are praying so you can watch what God does, and remain grateful whether you get the outcome you wanted or do not.

How can you better be in the practice of prayer?

_____

_____

_____

_____

_____

_____

_____

_____

_____

_____

_____

_____

_____

Love Everyone

And may the Lord cause you to increase and overflow with love for one another and for everyone, just as we also do for you.

—1 THESSALONIANS 3:12

Like the Thessalonians, we are called to love one another. Have you ever noticed, though, that some people are easier to love than others? People who are nice and respectful are easy to love. People who are fun and always in a good mood are also easy to love. But, what about people who are mean, moody, and no fun to be around? What about those who are different from us? How are we to act towards the person who hurts us? In all of these less than desirable situations, we are to love. If you are void of love towards those people who are hard to love, ask the Lord to increase your love for them. He will do it because He is love.

Do you need the Lord to increase your love for someone?

_____

_____

_____

_____

_____

_____

_____

_____

_____

_____

_____

_____

_____

_____

Rejection

**For God has not called us to impurity but to sanctification.
Therefore, the person who rejects this does not
reject man, but God, who also gives you His Holy Spirit.**

—1 THESSALONIANS 4:7–8

Sanctification is a big word. It means to become holy. As a Christian, you are called by God to live a holy life. Choosing an unholy or impure life is a rejection of God and the Holy Spirit, whom He has given you until His return. The irony with your age and verse 8 is that girls can make wrong decisions out of their fear of rejection, yet the poor decision, in turn, ends up rejecting God. Worrying over your rejection contributes to God's rejection. God calls you to be concerned about His rejection, from when you do the wrong thing, rather than being concerned about your rejection from when you do the right thing.

When have you felt rejected?

Suit Up

**But since we belong to the day, we must be serious
and put the armor of faith and love on our chests,
and put on a helmet of the hope of salvation.**

—1 THESSALONIANS 5:8

As a Christian, you belong to the light, or the day. You
no longer walk in darkness. Since you belong to the day,
you must suit up with faith, love, and hope. These three
virtues are considered armor, which should signal to you
that you are in a battle. The battle is between darkness
and light. As a child of light, darkness will make attacks
on you. Remember to suit up in your armor every day.
Your armor will protect you in combat against darkness.
Pay attention to where your armor goes on your body.
Faith and love are placed over your chest to protect
your heart, and hope is placed on your head to protect
your thoughts.

Do you ever think you're fighting a battle every day? How does that make you feel?

_____

_____

_____

_____

_____

_____

_____

_____

_____

_____

_____

_____

_____

Remember and Practice

Therefore, brothers, stand firm and hold to the traditions you were taught, either by our message or by our letter.

—2 THESSALONIANS 2:15

I am very nostalgic. It is important to me that my children experience the same traditions that I experienced when I was a child. I like that my sons have memories, like I do, of eating the same meal at Thanksgiving, having the same Christmas breakfast year after year, falling asleep with their miniature Christmas trees lit in their rooms, and eating packed snacks at the pool in the warmth of the summer sun.

There are also many traditions in the Christian faith. Easter, Christmas, communion, baptisms, weddings, and corporate worship are a few of those traditions. We are to stand firm in our Christian traditions, celebrating and worshipping with other believers. Being a part of a church allows us to stand firm and practice the traditions of our faith.

What are your favorite traditions?

Get Busy with Your Own Life

For we hear that there are some among you who walk irresponsibly, not working at all, but interfering with the work of others. Now we command and exhort such people by the Lord Jesus Christ that quietly working, they may eat their own food.

—2 THESSALONIANS 3:11–12

These verses may sound strange to you upon first reading them, but they are very applicable to your age. Girls spend a lot of time and energy focusing on other people and discussing their business, when it is really none of their business. These verses address such behavior. Interfering with other people's business is called irresponsible. Are you being irresponsible with your time? Do you spend any time behind a screen tracking what other people are doing? Do you spend any time talking at school about the latest gossip? If so, then take the advise of verse 12 and eat from your own table. Be concerned with what is on your "plate" and not your neighbor's.

Did you spend more time today thinking about your own actions or someone else's?

48

Who Are You Responsible For?

Brothers, do not grow weary in doing good.

—2 THESSALONIANS 3:13

My boys are three and five years of age. They love telling on each other. When one brother is acting badly, the other brother lets me know. They like pointing out each other's behavior or mistakes to make themselves look better. The motive of a tattletale is not just to get the other person in trouble, but to draw attention to how well they are doing compared to the person who messed up. When one of my boys tells on the other, I ask the informant this question— Who are you responsible for? I want him to concentrate on himself and his own behavior, not on his brother's.

Sometimes, the misbehavior of others can cause you to grow weary. You see peers get away with bad behavior at school, and you stop and ask yourself: What is the point in trying to be good? Instead of asking that question, ask yourself whom you are responsible for. Your responsibility as a Christian is to focus on yourself and not what others around you are doing. Do not grow weary in doing or being good. Remember, your standard is God, not other people.

Who or what makes it hard for you to stay the course in doing the right thing?

Tell the Future Generations

We must not hide them from their children,
but must tell a future generation the praises of the Lord,
His might, and the wonderful works He has performed.

—PSALM 78:4

Psalm 78 is a song by Asaph. Asaph, like King David, was a songwriter. In Psalm 78, Asaph traces the wonders of God beginning with the covenant with Jacob, and then moving backwards in time to how God rescued the Israelites from Egypt and provided for them in Sinai, and the song ends with mentioning King David. The song begins by saying, "We must tell a future generation the praises of the Lord." When you come into a relationship with Christ, you are signing on to being a storyteller of all His mighty works recorded for you in Scripture. You now have a responsibility to tell the future generations about the wondrous works of the Lord—the ones told about in His Word and the ones from your own life. Tell God's stories to your children, your grandchildren, and the generations behind you.

Is there someone in your life who needs to hear God's stories today?

_____

_____

_____

_____

_____

_____

_____

_____

_____

_____

_____

_____

_____

There Are Two Paths

For wisdom will enter your mind, and knowledge will delight your heart. Discretion will watch over you, and understanding will guard you, rescuing you from the way of evil— from the one who says perverse things, from those who abandon the right paths to walk in ways of darkness.

—PROVERBS 2:10–13

As a Christian, you are to walk on the path of wisdom and not on the path of darkness. The wise path contains knowledge. It is a pleasant path, and being on it keeps you from the other path of darkness. People on the path of darkness talk perverted and forsake the path of wisdom. They choose to be on the path of darkness because they rejoice in doing evil (Proverbs 2:14). Choosing the path of wisdom protects you from such people because the two paths do not cross.

If you were to draw a picture of the paths of wisdom and darkness, how would they look different?

_____

_____

_____

_____

_____

_____

_____

_____

_____

_____

_____

_____

_____

Embrace Discipline

**Do not despise the Lord's instruction, my son,
and do not loathe His discipline; for the Lord disciplines
the one He loves, just as a father, the son he delights in.**

—PROVERBS 3:11–12

Getting in trouble can feel shameful and embarrassing. Have you ever had your name called over the intercom to come to the front office? Even if it is a non-disciplinary call to the office, you can still feel your face turn red. But, when you are in a disciplinary related situation at school or at home, a surreal sinking feeling overtakes your gut and, as much as you want to tell yourself it is just a dream, you realize—I've been caught!

Scripture, however, tells us to welcome discipline and reproof, not resist it or ridicule the people enforcing it. God disciplines out of love, always having our best interest in mind. He does not want to shame us but change us.

Write out a prayer below and ask for an open heart that can learn from discipline.

_____

_____

_____

_____

_____

_____

_____

_____

_____

_____

_____

_____

_____

Guard Your Heart

**Guard your heart above all else,
for it is the source of life.**

—PROVERBS 4:23

At some point, you have to plug into an outlet any piece of technology you own or any appliance you use. From that outlet flows electricity that your electronics need in order to power on. Think of your heart as an outlet. From your heart flows life. What you allow to plug into you will affect your quality of life. An outlet does not have an option in what it gives its energy to, but you do. Do not "charge" bad relationships or unwise decisions. They will deplete life and energy from your heart.

What do you need to stop "charging"? An ungodly friendship? A bad habit?

Train

But have nothing to do with irreverent and silly myths. Rather, train yourself in godliness, for the training of the body has a limited benefit, but godliness is beneficial in every way, since it holds promise for the present life and also for the life to come.

—1 TIMOTHY 4:7–8

Anyone who regularly exercises can attest to feeling stronger from working out. Exercising helps us gain physical strength and mental clarity. The one thing that Paul points out in his letter to Timothy that exercise cannot do is benefit us in the life to come. Exercise helps us maintain weight and feel better overall, but it helps us now in the present life, not the life to come. Getting our bodies physically fit is important, but a fit body is not what allows us to enter the kingdom of heaven. We need to train ourselves in godliness with the same intensity that we train our bodies when we exercise. The difference is that godliness promises to benefit us in the life to come and exercising does not.

Would you rather exercise physically or spiritually? Why are both important?

_____

_____

_____

_____

_____

_____

_____

_____

_____

_____

_____

_____

_____

54

Content

But godliness with contentment is a great gain.

—1 TIMOTHY 6:6

Christians are to be Christlike. We should reflect to this world what it looks like to love and follow Christ. We are to be godly, holy, and set apart because our God is holy. Training ourselves in godliness requires discipline. Godliness may require us to say "no" when everyone else is saying "yes." The key to disciplining ourselves in godliness, though, is to pray for contentment. If we say "no" without being content, then we will not last long in our stance. We gain much when we say "no" because we genuinely want to set ourselves apart from the crowd.

When have you had to say "no" to the world?

_____

_____

_____

_____

_____

_____

_____

_____

_____

_____

_____

_____

_____

Content with Less

For we brought nothing into the world,
and we can take nothing out. But if we have
food and clothing, we will be content with these.

—1 TIMOTHY 6:7–8

On survival reality shows, fire and shelter are always the first two necessities the survivalists try to obtain. They work with what little they are given and what little they find. These shows remind me that the bare necessities of staying alive are minimal.

Our world teaches us differently. Our world teaches that each driver in a household needs a car, each wardrobe should include the latest fashion, and each piece of technology should be the most updated. God teaches us in his Word that none of the hype about the newest, latest, and most current matters because we cannot take any of it with us. When we hold onto material goods with our fists clinched, we will never learn contentment because we will always want the newest and the brightest. What we need to learn is being content with less.

List ten "necessities" you own that many people in other countries don't have.

_____

_____

_____

_____

_____

_____

_____

_____

_____

_____

_____

_____

Pursue the Godly

But you, man of God, run from these things, and pursue righteousness, godliness, faith, love, endurance, and gentleness.

—1 TIMOTHY 6:11

Paul is urging Timothy to run from the desire to want more. As girls, we can learn from this lesson. We want the latest style of jeans, the newest boots, the name brand purses, and the most popular accessories. It is not wrong to have any of these material goods as long as we can keep the perspective that they do not add to our value.

God values us just as we are and desires that we crave godly characteristics rather than craving the things that money brings. He wants us to pursue things of God not things of gold because He knows that ultimately only He can satisfy us.

How is God more satisfying than material items?

Hope in God

Instruct those who are rich in the present age not to be arrogant or to set their hope on the uncertainty of wealth, but on God, who richly provides us with all things to enjoy.

—1 TIMOTHY 6:17

I am all for dreaming big because God is a big God. There is, though, a certain element of reality that is needed in our hopes and dreams. Our dreams can be big, but we must not set them so large that we can never attain them.

God cautions us about one dream in particular. He warns us about the dream of becoming wealthy. God says that wealth is uncertain. It can go as easily as it came. God, however, never leaves us and provides for us with more care than money ever could. Our hopes and dreams need to center around the One who is our ultimate provider.

Is wealth a part of your biggest dream for your life?

Be Generous

Instruct them to do what is good, to be rich in good works, to be generous, willing to share.

—1 TIMOTHY 6:18

"It's mine!" is a phrase that I often hear exclaimed when my boys are arguing over toys. They each try to claim ownership over the toy at the center of the fight. They truly believe that if the toy is in their possession and they claimed it first, then it is theirs. In the midst of their dispute, I remind them that nothing is ours and that everything belongs to God. Oddly enough, this true statement causes them to pause and begin working out a trade of some sort.

God owns everything because He is the creator of everything. He is the One who brought forth light, created atmosphere, and started life. All that we have comes from God. As Owner, He requires us to be generous with what He gives us. Doing good deeds and being generous reflect a heart that recognizes God as Owner of everything.

Do you find it easy or hard to be generous?

Fearless

For God has not given us a spirit of fearfulness, but one of power, love, and sound judgment.

—2 TIMOTHY 1:7

When you were a little kid, you probably had a few bad dreams that left you full of fear when you awoke. Hopefully your parents were there to comfort you and assure you that you didn't need to be afraid. Now that you're older, you will face different fears, bigger fears, and you will need to decide how you will face them and who will help you through. One fear you might have is *How can I really live for God in this world and serve Him no matter what? What if I mess it all up?* Second Timothy 1:7 reassures you that you can be brave—God has blessed you with many gifts, and He will use them.

Spiritual maturity often comes with some scary challenges. Whatever your fear is, you can know that God will stand with you as you face it. He can give you wisdom to decide the right path and courage to deal with whatever or whoever tries to tempt you off that path.

Is it comforting to you to know that God is with you when you're scared?

_____

_____

_____

_____

_____

_____

_____

_____

_____

_____

_____

_____

_____

Pursue Righteousness

Flee from youthful passions, and pursue righteousness, faith, love, and peace, along with those who call on the Lord from a pure heart.

—2 TIMOTHY 2:22

Youthful passions include things like wanting to be popular, wanting to be in the middle of drama, and wanting the latest fad, game, or Apple product so you can brag about it. God tells you to flee such desires. How do you escape these desires when other young people, who run towards these desires, surround you? Paul answers this question by using the verb *pursue*. You must chase after the things of God in order to flee the things of the world. You cannot remain in neutral while the rest of your friends run after youthful passions. If you do, you will get caught in their current. You have to kick it in gear and swim upstream against the current of youthful passions.

Fill in the blank: "I really want a _____." Is your answer a godly desire or a worldly desire?

Keeping the End in Sight

For the grace of God has appeared with salvation for all people, instructing us to deny godlessness and worldly lusts and to live in a sensible, righteous, and godly way in the present age, while we wait for the blessed hope and appearing of the glory of our great God and Savior, Jesus Christ.

—TITUS 2:11–13

It helps to familiarize myself with a path when I am running a long distance. To know the course helps me as I run because I know there is an end to my running. The same is true when I drive long distances. A blue dot on the map on my phone, which signifies my location, keeps me motivated as I watch it inch closer to my final destination.

In life you have an end to your race. As a Christian, your final destination is eternity with God. God calls you to run your race with the end in sight. As you wait on Christ's return, deny godlessness and worldly lusts. Think about the promise of your Savior's return, and let that motivate you to live sensibly, righteously, and godly.

When you face a hard challenge, does it help you to focus on the goal and reward?

Reserve Your Water

Drink water from your own cistern, water flowing from your own well. Should your springs flow in the streets, streams of water in the public squares?

—PROVERBS 5:15–16

Marriage is the context of these verses. "Drinking water from your own cistern" means to keep intimacy in the marriage. Think about this in regards to young people, who are not married, and what they post on social media. Images that are meant only for a spouse's eyes get taken and posted for the public. The people who are posting such intimate pictures are letting their "springs flow in the streets." They are sharing what is meant for their spouse with other people.

One day when you are a wife, you will give yourself to your husband, not the public. Since you might be someone's spouse one day, begin reserving for him now what belongs to him in the future.

What are some questions to ask yourself before taking photos and posting them on social media?

A Girl of Few Words

**When there are many words, sin is unavoidable,
but the one who controls his lips is wise.**

—PROVERBS 10:19

God made girls vocal. We have a need to use up more words in a day than guys. It is like we start each day with a bank filled with words, and we spend the day depleting the bank. Take a look at your word bank. What words are in it? Are your words uplifting or cutting? Do they revolve around drama or encouraging others? Do they gossip about others or praise God?

As Christians, we know we need to control what words we use and when we use them. There are times when we should say little or nothing at all.

Think about your day. Were there times when you said too much or chose the wrong words?

_____

_____

_____

_____

_____

_____

_____

_____

_____

_____

_____

_____

_____

_____

Slow to Anger

My dearly loved brothers, understand this: Everyone must be quick to hear, slow to speak, and slow to anger, for man's anger does not accomplish God's righteousness.

—JAMES 1:19–20

As a Christian, God is sanctifying you. That means you are in a constant state of being purified by God. He wants to transform you more and more to where you look like His Son. Something that stands in the way of this purification process is anger. Anger does not make you look more like Jesus. It does not accomplish God's work of sanctification.

There seems to be a connection in verse 19 between anger, speaking, and listening. Based off of my experience, I speak words that I should not when I am angry. And if my anger is directed at another person, I would be less angry with that person if I stopped to listen to what the person was trying to say.

Anger ablaze in us keeps us from looking like Jesus. We need to squelch the anger that burns in us by listening and being quiet.

What is a good prayer for when you are trying to control your anger?

Apply What You Hear

Because if anyone is a hearer of the word and not a doer, he is like a man looking at his own face in a mirror. For he looks at himself, goes away, and immediately forgets what kind of man he was.

—JAMES 1:23–24

When you get ready in the morning, you walk out of the bathroom knowing how you look, and when you want to re-examine how you look at school, you head to the bathroom to look again in a mirror. If you looked in a mirror after lunch and saw a piece of your lunch stuck between your front teeth, you would remedy the problem before returning to class. You would not want to interact with others while something was stuck in your teeth. That would be embarrassing!

Applying God's Word in our lives is like checking ourselves in the mirror. We examine what we see, go about our day remembering and applying what we read, and then we go back to the mirror of God's Word to re-examine ourselves. And when we find things stuck in our heart that should not be there, we ask God to pick them out.

What are some ways you can refocus on God's Word throughout the day?

Anti-Pollution

Pure and undefiled religion before our God and Father is this: to look after orphans and widows in their distress and to keep oneself unstained by the world.

—JAMES 1:27

We all know that it is good to take care of the environment. We should recycle what we can, watch the exhaust from our cars, turn lights off when we are not using them, and so on. As Christians, we need to care even more about the pollution that can affect our lives. We need to watch what exhaust from the world we let into our minds and hearts because, as Christians, we are called to be "green." Rather than letting the pollution of the world into our lives, we should impact the world with our cleanliness.

Are there any habits, apps, movies, or songs in your life that God might consider "pollution"?

Merciful

For judgment is without mercy to the one who hasn't shown mercy. Mercy triumphs over judgment.

—JAMES 2:13

You draw conclusions about people every day. When you draw a negative conclusion about a person, it is easy to move into a state of judging her. Judgments about her run ramped in your heart, and there is no room for mercy.

God reminds us in James 2 that He will judge a person who judges others. Instead of judging, we are to show mercy. There are times when people may deserve the judgment we want to give them, but holding back from giving them the judgment they deserve is being merciful. After all, God was merciful toward us when Christ took on Himself the judgment we deserve and instead credited His righteousness to us.

Why is it hard to offer mercy to someone who deserves judgment instead?

_____

_____

_____

_____

_____

_____

_____

_____

_____

_____

_____

_____

_____

Faith with Works

In the same way faith, if it doesn't have works, is dead by itself. But someone will say, "You have faith, and I have works." Show me your faith without works, and I will show you faith from my works.

—JAMES 2:17–18

Noah, Abraham, Isaac, and Moses are some of the Old Testament people who are listed in Hebrews 11 as living by faith. They believed God and out of that belief, they accomplished their works. The works they accomplished were done by faith they had in God.

Old Testament believers trusted in the promise of the Messiah to come, and we trust in the promised Messiah who has come. Like the people of faith in the Old Testament, we are saved through faith by the grace of God. And like Old Testament believers, our works are accomplished through our faith and because of our faith. We are not saved because of our good works, but our good works flow from our saving faith.

Which Old Testament believer do you admire the most? Why?

_____

_____

_____

_____

_____

_____

_____

_____

_____

_____

_____

_____

_____

_____

The Tongue

So too, though the tongue is a small part of the body, it boasts great things. Consider how large a forest a small fire ignites. And the tongue is a fire. The tongue, a world of unrighteousness, is placed among the parts of our bodies. It pollutes the whole body, sets the course of life on fire, and is set on fire by hell.

—JAMES 3:5–6

The beginning of James 3 describes two large objects controlled by small parts. A horse, though a powerful animal, is controlled by a bit in his mouth. A ship is a massive vessel, yet a little rudder guides it. These descriptions are a comparison to how our small tongues control our entire body. Our words will either guide us in the right or wrong direction. Just like a tiny spark can ignite a forest fire, our tongues can detonate all sorts of explosions.

We need to tame our tongues so we do not pollute the world with the debris left behind by our words.

How does your tongue get you into trouble the most? Gossip? Complaining? Unkind words?

_____

_____

_____

_____

_____

_____

_____

_____

_____

_____

_____

_____

_____

_____

From Bitter to Sweet

Praising and cursing come out of the same mouth. My brothers, these things should not be this way.

—JAMES 3:10

A few days after Moses led the Israelites through the Red Sea, the Israelites started complaining in the wilderness because they were thirsty and needed water. They came to Marah where there was water, but they could not drink the water because it was bitter. Moses prayed to God about what to do, and God showed him a tree and told him to take a stick from the tree and throw it in the water. The water became sweet and drinkable. Just as God changed the condition of the water at Marah, He wants to change the condition of our hearts so that our bitter speech changes into sweet speech. He does not want both praise to Him and bitter speech about others to come out of the same mouth.

How does it feel to be around someone whose words are constantly bitter and negative?

Made in God's Likeness

**We praise our Lord and Father with [our tongue],
and we curse men who are made in God's likeness with it.**

—JAMES 3:9

James 3 tells us that praising and cursing should not flow from the same mouth. We should not speak badly about someone at school on Monday and Tuesday then turn around and praise God at youth group on Wednesday. James 3:9 reminds us that the person we curse is made in the image of God. Each human being resembles God, so when we speak poorly about someone, we are speaking poorly about God. It is like when my children express displeasure in a meal that I prepare and place before them. I take it personally because I feel like they are expressing displeasure in me.

We need to recognize the thumbprint of God on the people we talk about and realize that cursing them is expressing displeasure in God who created them.

Do you struggle with speaking well of certain people in your life?

_____

_____

_____

_____

_____

_____

_____

_____

_____

_____

_____

_____

Order

For where envy and selfish ambition exist, there is disorder and every kind of evil.

—JAMES 3:16

My closet reflects the busyness of my life. If I have a lot going on in my life and every hour in the day is accounted for, then my closet is usually a wreck. I leave clothes on the floor as I race out the door, and I do not hang my clothes up when I come home exhausted. The disorder of a wrecked closet is a good image of what our lives look like when we become envious or selfish in our motives. When we are selfishly striving for significance or are allowing jealousy to take root in our hearts, we become busy with those things and do not pay attention to ordering our lives, and they become a wreck of a mess.

Which part of your life is the most orderly?
Which part is more likely to be a wreck?

You Are Not of the World

If you were of the world, the world would love you as its own. However, because you are not of the world, but I have chosen you out of it, the world hates you.

—JOHN 15:19

Before you became a Christian, you were of the world. Your thoughts and actions belonged to the world. But when God chose you out of the world and claimed you, you became His. You are on God's team now. You play for Him. He is your coach and the star player of the team. The thing you need to know is that the world, the other team, hates you because it hates Him. Their hate hung Him on the cross so do not expect them to protect or like you.

Who in your life are your "God's team" teammates? Who is on the other team?

_____

_____

_____

_____

_____

_____

_____

_____

_____

_____

_____

_____

_____

The Spirit Speaks

When the Spirit of truth comes, He will guide you into all the truth. For He will not speak on His own, but He will speak whatever He hears. He will also declare to you what is to come.

—JOHN 16:13

As a Christian, you will learn to trust the Holy Spirit inside you. You will feel Him tug on your heart to take up for people who cannot defend themselves. You will hear Him whisper "Be careful" or "Watch out" before you make decisions. He will nudge your heart sometimes and convict you at other times. He will have you walk out of certain movies, walk away from certain situations, and walk toward certain people. He is a voice you need to train your ear to listen to because He speaks from your Father.

When have you felt the Holy Spirit guiding you?

Never Return to Your Old Ways

As obedient children, do not be conformed to the desires of your former ignorance.

—1 PETER 1:14

Little children seem to gravitate towards things that are dangerous. They like wires, cords, sharp objects, and lit burners. A mom, who catches her child climbing up towards the cooktop with his hand extended to touch the burner, will yell for her child not to touch the burner as she races over to him. The child learns to obey his mom and never go near the cooktop again. He learns this discipline because he knows that his mom loves him and is looking out for him, and out of love for her, he obeys, never to return to his old ways.

You are that child, and like the mom, God wants to rescue you from pain that can be prevented, but you have to be obedient. You have to listen to God's voice as he instructs you, and out of love for Him, obey Him and never return to your old ways.

What dangers is God trying to protect you from?

_____

_____

_____

_____

_____

_____

_____

_____

_____

_____

_____

_____

_____

76

Treated with Honor

**Husbands, in the same way, live with your wives
with an understanding of their weaker nature
yet showing them honor as coheirs of the grace of life,
so that your prayers will not be hindered.**

—1 PETER 3:7

You are a young girl, and this verse addresses husbands, so you might be wondering what this verse has to do with you. The answer is a lot. In this verse lies the hope of who you want to marry one day. You want to marry a man who shows you honor, who treats you as an equal, and who recognizes you as an equal inheritor of God's grace. You want to marry a man who holds the door for you, stands up for you when you enter a room, asks for your opinions, and values your opinions.

As women, we are not as physically strong as men. We also have certain sensitivities that men do not have. You want to marry a man who understands this about you but does not treat you like you are weak because of it.

Do not settle for less than being honored—in your future marriage, in your dating relationships, and in your friendships with other guys.

How do you want your future husband to treat you?

Give a Blessing

Now finally, all of you should be like-minded and sympathetic, should love believers, and be compassionate and humble, not paying back evil for evil or insult for insult but, on the contrary, giving a blessing, since you were called for this, so that you can inherit a blessing.

—1 PETER 3:8–9

It is in our nature to bite back when bitten. If a girl insults us or makes fun of us, we will make it known that we do not care for her. We take her nasty behavior and either match it or one up it. God says rather than paying back insult for insult, give a blessing. Can you imagine a school where girls do not pay back insult for insult or rumor for rumor? Can you picture a school where girls do not purposely snub each other and hurt each other's feelings? Can you conceive not saying anything negative on Monday about a friend who did not let you sit with her at the game Friday night? Rather than carrying that weight with you through the weekend, what if you let it go? Rather than talking about a girl who wronged you, what if you decided not to say anything negative about her? You just might be the one to stop the domino effect of nastiness.

Who needs a blessing from you?

_____

_____

_____

_____

_____

_____

_____

_____

_____

_____

_____

_____

_____

Be Ready

Always be ready to give a defense to anyone who asks you for a reason for the hope that is in you.

—1 PETER 3:15

As a Christian, people will notice things about your life that do not make sense to them. They will want to know why you do not cuss or gossip. They will want to know why you are nice to everyone, why you obey your parents, and why you are so happy. If they ask you why, and you tell them it is because of Jesus, be ready to answer the question that will immediately follow. They will want to know why you believe and hope in Christ and why they should believe it too. Are you ready to answer that question?

What is your answer? Why do you believe in Christ?

_____

_____

_____

_____

_____

_____

_____

_____

_____

_____

_____

_____

_____

_____

_____

Be Perfect

Be perfect, therefore, as your heavenly Father is perfect.

—MATTHEW 5:48

Let me save you some time. You cannot be perfect. You will never be perfect until Christ's return. Why would Jesus give a command we could not follow? In fact, why does Jesus give us commands when we are incapable of keeping any of them? Jesus wants us to see our need for Him in the face of each command that He perfectly kept. God gives us His standard for living through the person of Christ. When we are found in Christ's perfect righteousness, we are seen as righteous. Though we cannot be perfect as our Father is perfect, we can be found in Christ's perfection.

What one way can you be more like Christ this week?

_____

_____

_____

_____

_____

_____

_____

_____

_____

_____

_____

_____

_____

_____

Love One Another

By this all people will know that you are My disciples, if you have love for one another."

—JOHN 13:35

When people love each other well, they create strong youth groups, churches, schools, and communities. Strong youth groups have students who, out of love, cross over the boundaries created by cliques. Strong churches have members who take care of each other in times of need or plenty. Strong schools have parents and students who build community by supporting each other and the school.

You have a great opportunity to build community in your youth group, church, and school by loving well the people God has placed in your life. As you connect with other believers who share your same passion for crossing barriers with love, your communities will be unbreakable.

What are some examples of love at your church? What about at school?

_____

_____

_____

_____

_____

_____

_____

_____

_____

_____

_____

_____

_____

_____

81

Produce Fruit

Every branch in Me that does not produce fruit He removes, and He prunes every branch that produces fruit so that it will produce more fruit.

—JOHN 15:2

The metaphor to the Christian life is quite simple. Jesus is the vine. We are the branches. Our lives should produce the fruit of the Spirit—love, joy, peace, patience, kindness, goodness, faithfulness, gentleness, and self-control. The only way to produce this fruit is to remain in Christ. As we remain in Him, He prunes us so that we will keep producing His fruit. Apart from Christ, our vine, we have no chance of bearing fruit.

How is your life more fruitful today than it was two years ago?

_____

_____

_____

_____

_____

_____

_____

_____

_____

_____

_____

_____

_____

Truth

Sanctify them by the truth; Your word is truth.

—JOHN 17:17

In this verse and the surrounding verses, Jesus is praying to the Father on behalf of His disciples. Jesus knows He is about to be arrested and put on trial, which makes this particular verse even more beautiful. Jesus, on His way to His death, asks God to make His disciples holy by the truth. The truth, Jesus says, is God's Word. We know from Scripture that Jesus is the Word in flesh. So, Jesus is asking that God make His disciples holy by *Him*. He knows that the death He is about to die is truth, and He asks God to sanctify His disciples by His death.

We, too, are in the process of being made holy. God makes us holy by Jesus, the Word of truth. We have to look constantly at the Truth of the cross to be sanctified.

How is God making your holy as you look to Jesus?

_____

_____

_____

_____

_____

_____

_____

_____

_____

_____

_____

_____

_____

_____

_____

In the Safari

Be serious! Be alert! Your adversary the Devil is prowling around like a roaring lion, looking for anyone he can devour. Resist him and be firm in the faith.

—1 PETER 5:8–9

Satan knows his time is limited. He knows the death and resurrection of Christ has chained him for now and that Christ's return will permanently confine him. Because of this, he prowls like a lion looking to devour whoever he can. Christians, therefore, must be on alert as if we were walking in the safari. We must be serious about the dangers of attack that surround us in our jungle, the world. When the enemy approaches us in an open field wanting to devour us, we must resist his deathly grip by standing firm in our faith. Having the spear of God's Word in our hands is essential.

How does reading the Bible protect us?

84

Walk Like Christ

This is how we know we are in Him: The one who says he remains in Him should walk just as He walked.

—1 JOHN 2:5–6

You have different traits from your parents. You may look like your mom, dance like your dad (that could either be tragic or cool depending on how your dad dances), or laugh like your mom. I have my dad's mind, skin, and coordination and some of my mom's creativity. Whatever is passed along to us from our parents, there is one trait we must bear from our heavenly parent. We are to walk like our Father. When we start walking differently from our Father, we need to look back in His Word at how His Son walked. Christ gives us the picture of what it looks like to walk like the Father.

How does your walk resemble Christ's?

_____

_____

_____

_____

_____

_____

_____

_____

_____

_____

_____

_____

_____

85

Walk in the Light

But the one who hates his brother is in the darkness, walks in the darkness, and doesn't know where he's going, because the darkness has blinded his eyes.

—1 JOHN 2:11

Think of the imagery of light and darkness. Darkness leaves a room the moment the smallest light is lit. Even a small night-light will illuminate an entire room at night. As Christians, we are the light that radiates in this dark world. We cannot brighten a dark world if we have no light. Scripture says that hatred extinguishes our light. The moment we let hatred into our hearts, we are like a candle that has been snuffed out. Our wick is no longer lit. Once hatred sets in our hearts, it overtakes us. Our lives become as misdirected as if we were walking in the dark. Hatred makes us unable to see and confused about where we are going.

We need to constantly examine our hearts for seeds of hatred so that we can continue to walk in the light.

How does hate make you feel?

_____

_____

_____

_____

_____

_____

_____

_____

_____

_____

_____

_____

_____

Love with Action

Little children, we must not love with word or speech, but with truth and action.

—1 JOHN 3:18

God calls Christians to love, but we are not to just talk about how we love, we are to demonstrate our love. If a friend tells us in confidence who she likes, we should love her by not spreading that news to another friend. We are taking action to not act. We are actively restraining from sharing the information of her crush with other people. If we tell our friend who has the crush that we love her, then what better way to demonstrate our love for her by keeping her news to ourselves.

How can you demonstrate your love for your friends?

87

Keep God's Commands

**For this is what love for God is: to keep His commands.
Now His commands are not a burden.**

—1 JOHN 5:3

I grew up with my grandparents living right behind me. Their house backed up to my family's house. Our two backyards were like one big backyard. My sister and I would constantly run back and forth between their home and ours. The only time we did not enjoy running over to their house was when our mom would ask us to get something from their garden. Now, this was not a burdensome request. The vegetables were already picked and bagged for us. All we were doing was bringing the bag back to our mom as she cooked in the kitchen. Out of love for my mom, I would listen to her request even when she asked me to run the errand while my favorite TV show was on, and this was before you could pause live TV so what you missed while you were out of the room, you just missed.

God asks us to do things all the time, and out of love for Him, we do what He asks. What He asks is not burdensome, and it is worth missing out on anything that we might think we need to see or experience.

What specific thing have you done for God lately?

_____

_____

_____

_____

_____

_____

_____

_____

_____

_____

_____

_____

_____

Listen to the Lord

Hallelujah! Happy is the man who fears the Lord, taking great delight in His commands.

—PSALM 112:1

We live in an age where we value what we have to say more than we value what other people have to say. This is why social media has taken off. We get to blast our thoughts, opinions, and updates for others to see and hear. We get to be seen and heard on the stage of the Internet. This is a disservice to us because the skill of listening is no longer being practiced, only the skill of "posting."

Christianity requires the practice of listening. Psalm 112 connects that listening to God in His Word brings us delight. Our life is full and happy when we listen to God. We must practice listening to Him as we read what He says in Scripture.

How can you be a better listener?

True Happiness

Happy are those who keep His decrees and seek Him with all their heart.

—PSALM 119:2

You seek to be happy. You seek after friends, popularity, the right look, talent, and good grades for your happiness. The problem is that seeking after these things will not make you happy. They might bring you happiness temporarily, but the happiness will not last. Even the best of friendships can bring hurts as well as happiness. Popularity evolves and changes, which is why you keep the hope of possibly getting in with the popular crowd. As soon as you attain the look that is "in," another style comes along. The position you worked so hard to get could be given to someone younger or new to your school who outshines your talent. And when it comes to grades, you cannot maintain a perfect score in each subject and have a life at the same time. But take hope! There is one thing you can seek after that will always fulfill you and never disappoint you. There is one thing about your life that will never change. There is one thing that will always keep you happy, and it is your relationship with Christ. Seeking Him in His Word will bring you happiness.

How does Christ bring you happiness?

_____

_____

_____

_____

_____

_____

_____

_____

_____

_____

_____

_____

_____

Study

I will meditate on Your precepts and think about Your ways.

—PSALM 119:15

Outside of the classroom, you probably spend your time studying lyrics, music, statistics, sports, news from social media, and your favorite TV shows. God wants you to come to His Word with the same astuteness and attention that you give to these other subjects. You are to meditate on His instructions laid out for you in Scripture. You are to study your Bible with the same intensity you study academics, sports, or entertainment.

How much screen time do you have a day? Do you give as much attention to God's Word as you give to your laptop, phone, or television?

Estimate your weekly screen time and Bible study time below. How do they compare?

_____

_____

_____

_____

_____

_____

_____

_____

_____

_____

_____

_____

_____

_____

How to Have a Full Life

May Your compassion come to me so that I may live, for Your instruction is my delight.

—PSALM 119:77

In this verse, God's compassion and His instruction are interchangeable. His compassion and instruction both bring us life, and His compassion and instruction are both our delight. God's compassion brought us life, and we take delight in knowing what His compassion did for us. The instruction God gives us in His Word also brings us life. We make wiser decisions, become less selfish, and gain counsel when we turn to the instruction of His Word, and the wise decisions, selflessness, and counsel, in turn, bring us a fuller life.

How do God's rules actually make your life happier?

_____

_____

_____

_____

_____

_____

_____

_____

_____

_____

_____

_____

_____

_____

You Are Remarkable

**For it was You who created my inward parts;
You knit me together in my mother's womb. I will praise
You because I have been remarkably and wonderfully made.
Your works are wonderful, and I know this very well.**

—PSALM 139:13–14

Remarkable is not the first word that comes to mind if a young girl were asked to describe herself. She might think she is physically or socially awkward, but not remarkable. She might think she is odd and peculiar, but not remarkable. The truth is that she is wonderfully made even if she cannot see it. God knit her inside of her mother, and God has a wonderful plan for her life.

If only you could realize how the things you take for granted about yourself actually show how wonderful God is! The more time you spend with your Maker, the more you will understand just how remarkable He is for making you the way you are.

Make a list of all the things your remarkable body does on its own {breathing, blinking, etc.}.

_____

_____

_____

_____

_____

_____

_____

_____

_____

_____

_____

_____

_____

Silence

Whoever shows contempt for his neighbor lacks sense, but a man with understanding keeps silent.

—PROVERBS 11:12

You know how hard it is to bite your tongue and not speak when everything inside you wants to say something. When you have news about someone you dislike, you want that news known. There is a satisfaction you get from the word getting out about this person. Wanting to stain someone's reputation lacks sense. God calls you instead to be considerate. Being kind and considerate means you shut your mouth and keep silent. Rather than spreading gossip, a wise girl keeps silent about news that could taint someone's reputation.

Do you enjoy being around someone who gossips?

_____

_____

_____

_____

_____

_____

_____

_____

_____

_____

_____

_____

_____

_____

Don't Look Like a Pig

A beautiful woman who rejects good sense is like a gold ring in a pig's snout.

—PROVERBS 11:22

Pigs are dirty animals, and it is with their snout that they prod around in the mud. Imagine a beautiful gold ring in a pig's snout getting dragged through the mud and through a trough of scraps as the pig gobbles his food. What a waste of a beautiful ring!

The image of a gold ring in a pig's snout represents a beautiful girl who rejects sound judgment. What a waste of beauty when a girl makes poor decisions. Her poor judgments drag her through the mud and tarnish her beauty.

Who in your life can help you make wise decisions?

_____

_____

_____

_____

_____

_____

_____

_____

_____

_____

_____

_____

_____

_____

95

Build Your Reputation

Every wise woman builds her house, but a foolish one tears it down with her own hands.

—PROVERBS 14:1

You are in the business of construction. At your age, you are building your reputation. The foundation to your reputation is your belief in Jesus. Every board that frames the structure is a decision you make, and each nail is your integrity. A wise woman makes good decisions that build her reputation as a Christian. She carefully constructs her character because she knows that her life should reflect Christ. A foolish woman takes a sledgehammer to her own reputation by the poor decisions she makes. In the end, she can only look to herself when she looks in the mirror and sees a dilapidated reputation.

What are some ways to protect your reputation?

Your Steps

**A man's heart plans his way,
but the Lord determines his steps.**

—PROVERBS 16:9

Notice that this proverb says a person has a plan. She does not leave the path of her life up to happenstance. She has a direction and a purpose. In her heart she plans the approach she wants to take. The Lord has the final say, but that does not mean that she sits around waiting on her course to fall out of the sky. She is proactive as she waits on the Lord. He is the determining factor in her course, but she is moving towards a goal as she waits on His direction.

Move towards your hopes and dreams, and as you pray, God will direct you the entire way.

What are your plans for the next two years?
What about the next five years?

_____

_____

_____

_____

_____

_____

_____

_____

_____

_____

_____

_____

_____

Your Motives

All a man's ways seem right to him, but the LORD evaluates the motives.

—PROVERBS 21:2

God is great at calling our bluff. If we say that we are going to bake a cake for our teacher because we like her, but really we want to butter up to her because we have a poor grade in the class, God knows the truth. We might fool our teacher and even ourselves, but God knows the true motive of our heart. Because God evaluates our motives, it is necessary to bring Him everything we do or think of doing. When we hand our plans to Him, He exposes our motives. When we realize that a particular motive is for our glory and not God's, then we should restructure our plan. Honestly, this way of living saves us time because we do not waste our time doing the things that only bring glory to us.

How often do you take your plans to God before you act?

_____

_____

_____

_____

_____

_____

_____

_____

_____

_____

_____

_____

_____

My Daily Bread

Keep falsehood and deceitful words far from me. Give me neither poverty nor wealth; feed me with the food I need.

—PROVERBS 30:8

The phrase "give us today our daily bread" is part of the Lord's Prayer recorded in Matthew 6. The meaning behind this part of the prayer is for the believer to trust God to give her what is necessary. The same thought is expressed in Proverbs 30:8 with the words "feed me with the food I need." We can tend to pray for things that aren't necessary, and focusing on God's provision for our daily needs helps us weed out the things we want but do not really need.

Dependence on God is a beautiful part of the Christian walk. We should turn to God for our daily needs just as the Lord's Prayer and Proverbs 30:8 suggest.

What daily necessities do you take for granted?

Your Heart

As water reflects the face, so the heart reflects the person.

—PROVERBS 27:19

As girls, we spend so much of our time worrying about how we look on the outside. We want our hair to stay straight on humid days, our make-up not to smear, and our clothes to be cute. Mirrors give us honest feedback of what we look like. If we pull our hair back in a ponytail, a mirror will not reflect that our hair is down. Mirrors give us a true picture of what we look like. In the same way, our hearts give us a true depiction of what we look like. What is going on in our hearts is a reflection of our character.

Take a long imaginary look at your heart. What do you see?

_____

_____

_____

_____

_____

_____

_____

_____

_____

_____

_____

_____

_____

Benediction

May the Lord of peace Himself give you peace always in every way. The Lord be with all of you.

—2 THESSALONIANS 3:16

A benediction is a public mention of a blessing, usually at the end of a worship service. In this verse, Paul gives his benediction to the Thessalonians at the end of his second letter to them.

My favorite benediction when I was growing up was the choir at my home church singing, "May the Lord bless you and keep you. The Lord make his face to shine upon you, and give you peace, and be gracious unto you." This benediction comes from Numbers 6:24–26, and it is what I leave you with. God is peace. As you seek Him, you will know peace. May He give you peace always and in every way. The Lord be with you.

How does God give us a peace that is different
from any other?

_____

_____

_____

_____

_____

_____

_____

_____

_____

_____

_____

_____

_____